BRIGHT IDEA BOOKS

JORDAN Peele

by Samantha S. Bell

CAPSTONE PRESS
a capstone imprint

Bright Idea Books are published by Capstone Press
1710 Roe Crest Drive, North Mankato, Minnesota 56003
www.mycapstone.com

Library of Congress Cataloging-in-Publication Data
Library of Congress Cataloging-in-Publication Data is available on the Library of Congress website.
ISBN: 978-1-5435-5793-0 (library hardcover)
978-1-5435-6038-1 (paperback)
978-1-5435-5825-8 (eBook PDF)

Editorial Credits
Editor: Claire Vanden Branden
Designer: Becky Daum
Production Specialist: Colleen McLaren

Photo Credits
Alamy: Richard Ellis, 17; AP Images: Vince Bucci/Invision, cover; iStockphoto: TomasSereda, 11; Newscom: Byron Purvis/AdMedia, 18; Rex Features: Cindylou/Monkeypaw Prods./Martel & Roberts Prods./Kobal, 21, David Buchan/Variety, 8–9, David Fisher, 5, New Line Cinema/Principato-Young/Kobal, 24–25, Stephen Lovekin, 23; Shutterstock Images: CREATISTA, 30–31, Dfree, 26–27, Kathy Hutchins, 6–7, Kathy Hutchins, 14, lev radin, 12–13

Printed in the United States of America.
PA48

TABLE OF CONTENTS

CHAPTER 1

MAKING
History

Everyone in the crowd was standing and clapping. Jordan Peele just won an Academy Award.

Peele made a horror movie called *Get Out*. The movie won for Best Original Screenplay. Peele made history. He was the first African-American to win this award. Peele wrote and **directed** *Get Out*.

Peele with his Academy Award on March 4, 2018

Peele and the stars of *Get Out*, Daniel Kaluuya (left) and Allison Williams (right)

6

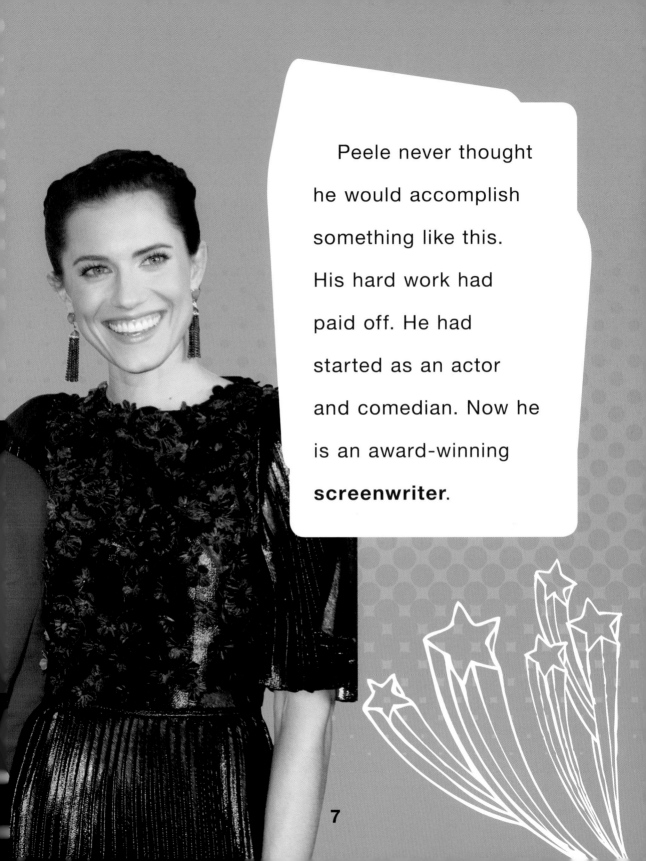

Peele never thought he would accomplish something like this. His hard work had paid off. He had started as an actor and comedian. Now he is an award-winning **screenwriter**.

Peele gave speeches after he won awards for *Get Out*.

A BIG HIT

Peele wanted to scare people. He wanted to make them think too. *Get Out* is about **racism**. The movie was a huge success. It made a lot of money. People loved it. The movie was also **nominated** for other awards.

THE ACADEMY AWARDS

The Academy Awards are the highest awards in film in the United States. Winners are given a gold statue. It is called an Oscar.

CHAPTER 2

GROWING Up

Peele was born on February 21, 1979. He is **biracial**. His mother is white. His father was African-American. This made Peele feel like an outsider sometimes. He was not sure where he fit in. His father left when Peele was young. Peele grew up with just his mother.

Peele grew up in New York City, New York.

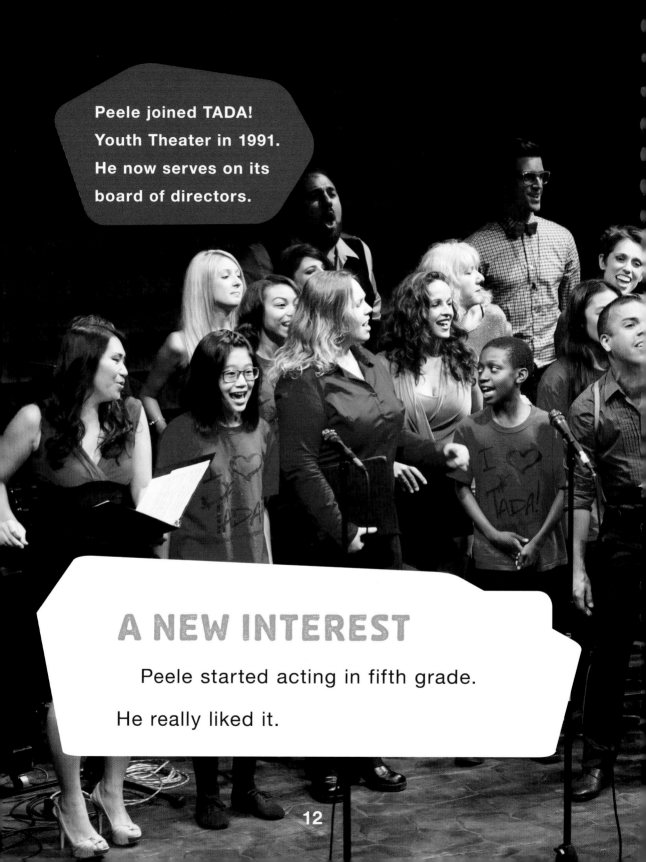

Peele joined TADA!
Youth Theater in 1991.
He now serves on its
board of directors.

A NEW INTEREST

Peele started acting in fifth grade.

He really liked it.

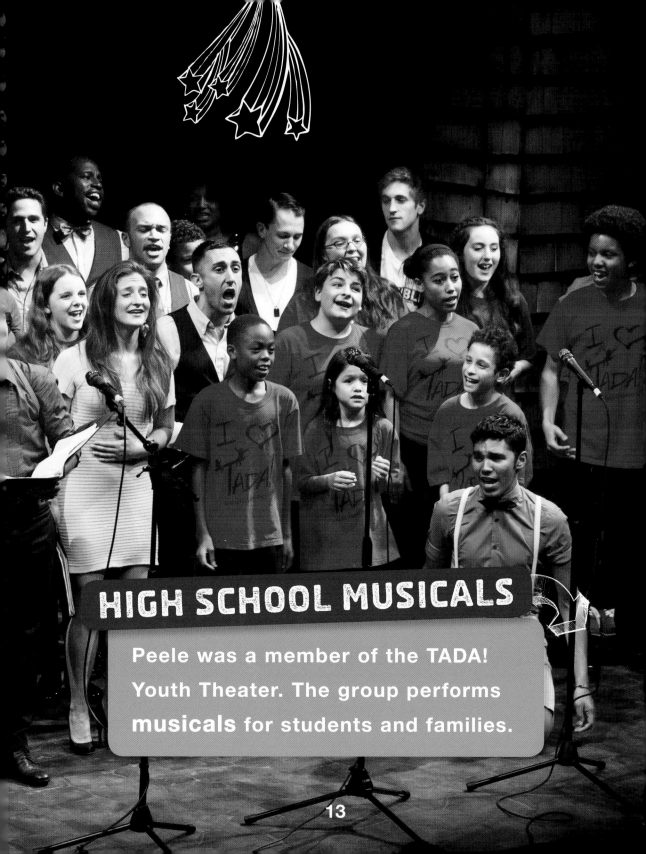

HIGH SCHOOL MUSICALS

Peele was a member of the TADA! Youth Theater. The group performs **musicals** for students and families.

Peele says that scary stories became his strength after he scared his classmates around a fire.

14

Sometimes Peele watched scary movies. They frightened him a lot. One day, he went on a school trip. The students sat around a campfire. Peele told scary stories to the other students. He found out he liked telling stories.

Peele had a dream at 13 years old. He wanted to win an Academy Award someday.

CHAPTER 3

A STRONG
Start

Peele often practiced speaking like other people as a child. He became good at **impersonations**.

After high school, Peele attended college. He went to Sarah Lawrence College in New York. Peele wanted to work with puppets. Then he began doing **improv**. He also liked doing comedy.

Peele decided to leave college. He wanted a career in comedy. He joined an improv group. The group traveled to Chicago to perform. There Peele met Keegan-Michael Key. Key was a comedian too. They became good friends.

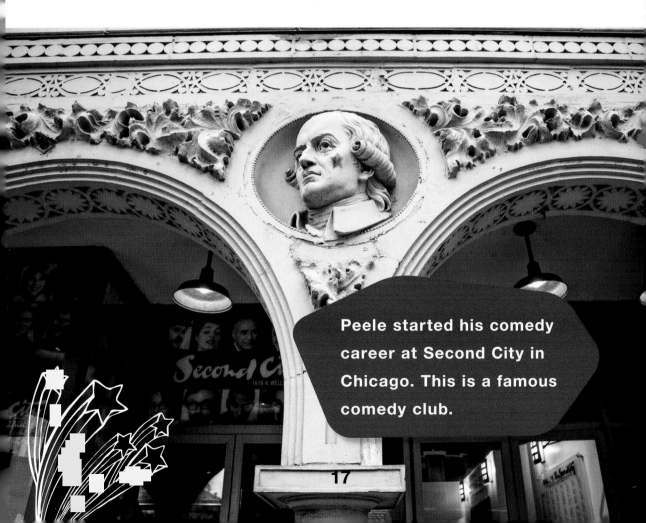

Peele started his comedy career at Second City in Chicago. This is a famous comedy club.

Key (left) and Peele enjoy making each other laugh.

A BIG BREAK

In 2003, Peele and Key both tried out for *MADtv*. This was a **sketch comedy** show that aired once a week. They were both hired.

Peele played many different people on the show. Some were celebrities. Some were musicians. He soon became a star on the show.

Peele often impersonated
President Barack Obama.

21

CHAPTER 4

COMEDY
Stars

MADtv ended five years later. The two friends started their own show in 2012. They called it *Key and Peele*. It aired on MTV.

The show covered things such as race and **gender**. It made viewers laugh. It also made them think about problems in the world. The show won several awards.

Key and Peele won an Emmy award in 2016 for *Key and Peele*. The award was for Outstanding Variety Sketch Series.

THE BIG SCREEN

Then Peele and Key wanted to make
their own movie. That dream came true
in 2016. They made an action comedy
called *Keanu*. Peele's second film was
Get Out. He realized he liked directing
more than acting.

Keanu made more than $20 million as of 2016.

25

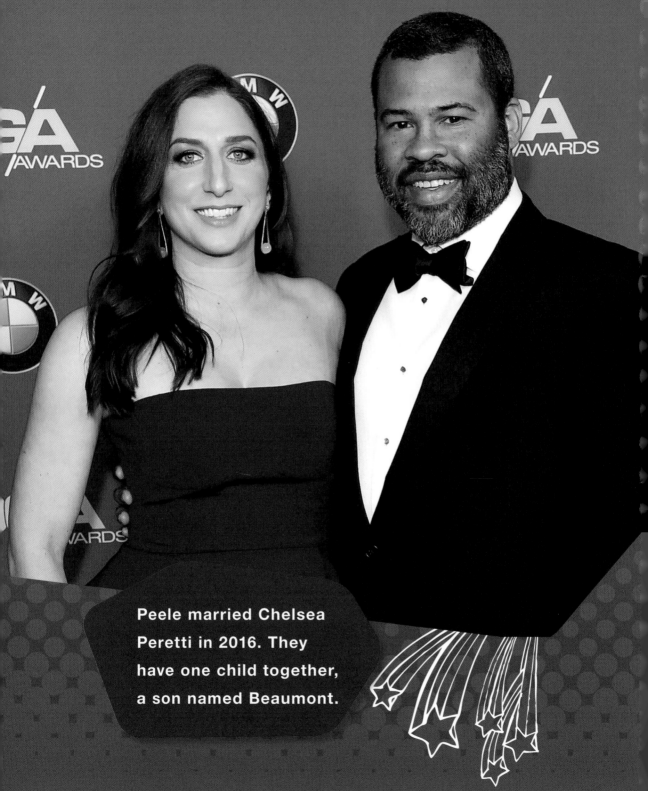

Peele married Chelsea Peretti in 2016. They have one child together, a son named Beaumont.

Now Peele has a new dream. He wants to make more scary movies. His movies will be frightening and funny. They will also cover real problems in the world.

MONKEYPAW PRODUCTIONS

Peele created his own **production company**. Its shows and movies will combine real-world problems with humor. It is called Monkeypaw Productions.

GLOSSARY

biracial
having parents of two different races

direct
to be in charge of actors and crew members for a movie, play, or musical

gender
the behaviors or traits usually associated with either males or females

impersonation
pretending to be another person

improv
a form of theater, often comedy, in which most or all of the performance is unplanned

musical
a play that tells a story with songs

nominated
to have been chosen as a candidate for something

production company
a company that provides money for TV shows or movies to be made

racism
the belief that certain races are superior to others

screenwriter
a person who writes scripts for movies, including instructions on how a movie should be acted and filmed

sketch comedy
a show that is made up of short funny stories

TIMELINE

1979: Jordan Peele is born.

2003: Peele meets Keegan-Michael Key.

2012: Peele and Key star in *Key and Peele* on MTV.

2016: Peele marries comedian Chelsea Peretti.

2017: Peele and Peretti have a baby boy named Beaumont Gino Peele.

2018: Peele's movie *Get Out* wins an Academy Award for Best Original Screenplay.

ACTIVITY

TRY IMPROV

Improv is a type of acting that does not use a script. Instead, the actors make up the scene as they go along. The scenes are usually funny.

30

You can try improv with your friends or family. First, choose two or more people to act out the scene. Everyone else will be the audience.

Next, have a person in the audience suggest a location, an action, an object, or a career. The actors must then use that suggestion to create the scene.

If you need any inspiration, check out other groups online. Improv4Kids puts videos of improv shows and comedy on YouTube. Ask an adult to help you find one of these videos on the company's YouTube channel.

FURTHER RESOURCES

Interested in acting? Try some of these scenes and plays:

Harbison, Lawrence. *The Best Scenes for Kids Ages 7–15*. Milwaukee, WI: Applause Theare & Cinema Books, 2015.

PBS Zoom Playhouse: Act Up and Put On a Play
https://pbskids.org/zoom/activities/playhouse

Wonder what improv looks and sounds like? Visit this website to see some kids in action:

http://www.thecomedykids.com

Want to practice improvising? Try this activity:

Bay Area Discovery Museum: Dubbing
https://creativitycatapult.org/activity/dubbing

INDEX